EXPLORE
HONEY
BEES!

Cindy Blobaum

Illustrated by Bryan Stone

Newest titles in the **Explore Your World!** Series

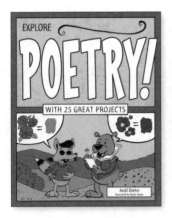

Check out more titles at www.nomadpress.net

Nomad Press
A division of Nomad Communications
10 9 8 7 6 5 4 3 2 1

This book was manufactured by Marquis Book Printing,
Montmagny Québec, Canada
June 2015, Job #109720

ISBN Softcover: 978-1-61930-290-7
ISBN Hardcover: 978-1-61930-286-0

Illustrations by Bryan Stone
Educational Consultant, Marla Conn

Questions regarding the ordering of this book should be addressed to
Nomad Press
2456 Christian St.
White River Junction, VT 05001
www.nomadpress.net

Printed in Canada.

For Phil, my beekeeping honey of a husband, and
Aunt Traci Henning, who first suggested I write about honey bees.

CONTENTS

Interested in primary sources? Look for this icon.

Use a smartphone or tablet app to scan the QR code and explore more about honey bees! You can find a list of URLs on the Resources page.

20,000,000 BCE:
Honey bees have changed into a more modern form.

100,000,000 BCE:
The first bee-like insects appear. We know this because the bodies of some early bees have been found trapped in amber.

8,000 BCE:
Humans draw a picture of their honey hunt on a cave wall in Valencia, Spain.

3,000–660 BCE:
Egyptians move mud and clay bee hives up and down the Nile. They record what they are doing in hieroglyphics on the walls of temples, tombs, and pottery.

1538 CE:
The Spanish take the first hives of European honey bees to South America.

384–322 BCE:
Greek and Roman writers and thinkers try to create new ways to manage bees.

1586:
Luiz Méndez de Torres, of Spain, first describes the largest bee as a female queen that lays the eggs.

1609:
Charles Butler, of England, identifies male drone bees.

1637:
Richard Remnant, of England, identifies the worker bees as females.

Timeline

1789:
Francis Huber, of Sweden, creates a moveable frame leaf hive. He is considered the father of modern bee science.

1850s:
Honey bees have spread from the East Coast of the United States all the way to California.

1638:
The Pilgrims bring the first honey bees to North America.

1851–1852:
Lorenzo Langstroth creates a moveable frame hive with a 3/8-inch bee space that is easy to make and use. He's called the father of American beekeeping.

1950s:
Brother Ada, an English monk, begins breeding bees that are resistant to diseases.

1854:
Dr. Johann Dzierzon, of Poland, discovers how royal jelly is made and used.

1973:
Karl von Frisch, an Austrian zoologist, is awarded a Nobel Prize for discovering why honey bees waggle dance.

2014:
U.S. President Barack Obama creates a task force to study why the number of honey bees has been dropping and what can be done about it.

1984:
Honey bees are taken aboard a NASA space shuttle. The bees construct a honeycomb while orbiting Earth.

v

THE BUZZ ABOUT HONEY BEES

When you go outside on a warm spring day, what do you see? It doesn't matter if you live in the city or the country, the trees will be leafy and green and flowers will be blooming. And where there are flowers, there are bees!

What do you know about honey bees? Have you ever watched one at work in a flower? Are you afraid honey bees will sting you? Do you eat products that come from honey bees, such as honey?

Honey bees are small but mighty **insects**. They live in **colonies** of thousands of bees. Honey bees work together to keep the colony alive and healthy.

WORDS to KNOW

insect: an animal that has three body parts, six legs, and its skeleton on the outside of its body. Many insects have wings. Grasshoppers, ants, ladybugs, and honey bees are all insects.

colony: a group that lives and works together.

1

nectar: a sweet fluid made by flowers that attracts insects.

pollen: a powder made by flowers that is needed for the flower to make a seed.

bee bread: a mixture of pollen, bee spit, and nectar.

royal jelly: a special food honey bees make to feed to the young bees.

Honey bees collect **nectar** and **pollen** from flowers. They use the nectar and pollen to make honey, **bee bread**, beeswax, and **royal jelly**. These are the basic things honey bees need to make their homes and feed their young.

HONEY BEES AND FLOWERS

When honey bees collect nectar and pollen, they are also helping the flowers. Flowers have the important job of making seeds that grow into new plants. They do this by moving pollen from one area of the flower to another, and by sending their pollen to other flowers. But flowers can't always get their pollen to the right place on their own. So they rely on help from honey bees!

Honey bees are covered in tiny hairs. When a honey bee lands on a flower, the pollen sticks to its hairs. As the honey bee moves around in the flower, it spreads the pollen.

Introduction

IT'S OFFICIAL

Every type of plant and animal has its own scientific name in Latin. This helps scientists all around the world, no matter what language they speak, make sure they are talking about the same type of plant or animal. The scientific name for honey bees is *Apis mellifera*. If you translate that into English, it means *honey-carrying bee*. Even if they are really carrying nectar and pollen, it's a great description of a honey bee!

Honey bees carry the pollen on them when they visit other flowers and spread it around there, too. With pollen in the right places, flowers can make their seeds.

pollinate: to transfer pollen from the male parts of flowers to the female parts so that flowers can make seeds.

WORDS to KNOW

What is your favorite fruit? Some plants, such as apples, peaches, pears, and watermelons, grow fruit around their seeds. Honey bees **pollinate** more than 100 types of plants that become food for us. Maybe one of these is your favorite!

DID YOU KNOW?

Many foods need honey bees or other insects to carry pollen from flower to flower. These include kiwis, cashews, watermelons, cantaloupes, cucumbers, lemons, limes, pumpkins, apples, mangoes, avocados, apricots, cherries, plums, almonds, peaches, pears, raspberries, blackberries, and blueberries.

3

hive: the place where bees live, lay eggs, and make food.

stinger: a sharp point at the end of some insects' bodies.

venom: poison given off by some animals and insects.

resin: a sticky liquid made by trees.

propolis: a sticky glue made by bees using tree resin.

WORDS to KNOW

HONEY BEES AND ANIMALS

The things honey bees make from nectar and pollen are good for lots of other creatures, not just honey bees. Many animals, such as bears, skunks, honey badgers, mice, and even other insects, try to move into **hives** to eat honey bee food and babies.

Female honey bees try to protect the hive against these creatures with **stingers** and **venom**. But some animals aren't bothered by stings. Sometimes these animals destroy the hive to get what they want, and then the honey bees have to start all over again by building a new hive.

People really like the things that honey bees make too. Honey tastes good mixed in tea, spread on toast, or used to make Sweet Snack Bars. Some people eat bee bread, royal jelly, and propolis because it makes them feel healthy. Beeswax is used to make candles, shine and protect wood furniture, and waterproof shoes.

DID YOU KNOW?

Bees collect a small amount of sticky **resin** from trees. They use this to make a special bee glue called **propolis**.

4

BEEKEEPING HISTORY

beekeeper: a person who raises bees.

WORDS to KNOW

People used to have to search for bee hives to get honey. Wild honey bees cleverly make their hives in hard-to-reach places, including caves, walls, and holes in trees. People often had to destroy the hives to get the honey bee products, and they got stung—a lot! To make it easier to get honey, people started making their own hives where honey bees could live. These people are called **beekeepers**.

Beekeepers protect the hives from other animals. They move the hives from place to place so the bees are close to blooming flowers. If the hives are in a place that gets cold, beekeepers might wrap them up in blankets to keep them warm.

WHAT BEE KEEPS YOU HEALTHY?

Vitamin Bee!

People learned to take just some of what the honey bees make, not all of it. This way, the honey bees don't have to start over by making a new hive. Instead, they can keep working at making honey, bee bread, beeswax, royal jelly, and propolis.

chemical: a substance that has certain features that can react with other substances.

climate: the average weather in an area during a long period of time.

DYING HONEY BEES

During the past several years, beekeepers all across the world have noticed that more honey bees than usual are dying. Why is this happening?

Scientists have a few ideas to explain why honey bees are having trouble. It could be that the **chemicals** people use to kill other insects are killing or hurting honey bees at the same time. Scientists know that honey bee colonies are getting attacked by tiny animals called mites. Honey bees are also having trouble because the **climate** across the world is changing.

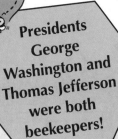

DID YOU KNOW?

Presidents George Washington and Thomas Jefferson were both beekeepers!

PESTICIDE

WHERE ARE ALL THE HONEY BEES?

Many people worry that too many honey bees are dying. What would the world be like if there were no honey bees? How would it change the way we eat? In 2014, President Barack Obama asked scientists to study what is happening to the honey bees. He wants to know what is hurting honey bees and how to help them. This study could help the honey bees that are kept in the White House garden and all of the honey bees you see flying around flowers in the park!

GOOD STUDY PRACTICES

Every good bee detective keeps a study journal! The first activity in this book is to make a Honey Bee Journal. As you read through this book and do the activities, keep track of your observations and record each step in a scientific method worksheet, like the one shown here. Scientists use the scientific method to keep their experiments organized.

Each chapter of this book begins with an essential question to help guide your exploration of honey bees.

Question: What are we trying to find out? What problem are we trying to solve?
Research: What do other people think?
Hypothesis/Prediction: What do we think the answer will be?
Equipment: What supplies are we using?
Method: What procedure are we following?
Results: What happened and why?

? ESSENTIAL QUESTION

Keep the question in your mind as you read the chapter. At the end of each chapter, use your Honey Bee Journal to record your thoughts and answers.

Some places are getting colder or wetter. Other places are having long **droughts**. When there isn't enough water, plants can't grow. Then the bees can't get what they need to make honey.

What do you want to learn about honey bees? There is no better time to bee-come a detective! By reading this book and doing the activities, you will learn all about honey bees and what they need to survive.

WORDS to KNOW

drought: a long period of time without rain in places that usually get rain.

ACTIVITY

HONEY BEE JOURNAL

Keep track of all you do and learn in a special Honey Bee Journal. As you add more pages, your journal will start to look like a flower!

SUPPLIES

* at least 10 sheets of thick paper
* ruler
* pencil
* highlighter marker
* hole punch
* brass paper fastener

1 Use the ruler and pencil to mark a 1-inch margin on two edges of each piece of paper. These two edges need to be next to each other, so choose either the top and a side or the bottom and a side.

2 Color the margins with the marker. Highlighters have fluorescent dye that can be seen by honey bees.

3 Punch a hole in the corner opposite the colored corner on each page. Push the brass paper fastener through the holes to hold the papers together. To make it look like a flower, fan the papers out in a circle.

4 On the top page, draw a picture of a honey bee. See the activity in Chapter 1 for step-by-step instructions.

5 For each activity or experiment you do, write your observations and results on one page in your journal. Label each page in the highlighted area.

CHAPTER 1
HONEY BEE BODIES

What does a honey bee look like? You might notice it has big eyes, wings, a fuzzy striped body, and many other **characteristics**! When you look at the characteristics of an animal's body, you are studying its **anatomy**. Every part of a honey bee's body helps it survive.

When humans are born, they look like little humans, but when insects are born, they usually look very different than the adults.

? ESSENTIAL QUESTION

How is a bee's body designed to do the work it's supposed to do? How is your body designed to do the work you do?

WORDS to KNOW

metamorphosis: the four major changes an insect goes through—egg, larva, pupa, adult.

larva: a young insect that has just hatched out of its egg and looks like a worm. Plural is *larvae*.

cocoon: a covering that some insects make around themselves to protect them while they grow.

pupa: a stage in an insect's life cycle when it changes from a larva into an adult. Plural is *pupae*.

EGG, LARVA, PUPA, ADULT

Like many other insects, honey bees go through four different life stages, called **metamorphosis.** All honey bees start out as eggs. It's the queen bee's job to lay eggs. When it's warm enough, she lays one egg per wax cell in a special area of the hive. She can lay between 1,000 and 2,000 eggs each day!

An egg hatches about three days after being laid. The baby bee, called a **larva**, looks like a small, white worm. Worker bees feed the cell up to 1,300 times a day. The larva eats and grows and sheds its skin for 5½ days. When the larva completely fills the bottom of the wax cell, the workers put in the last bit of food and cap the top with a piece of wax.

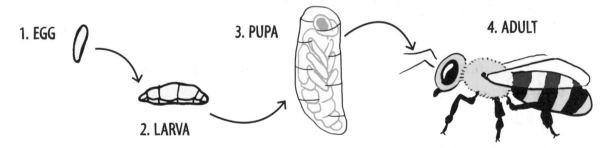

1. EGG 2. LARVA 3. PUPA 4. ADULT

Inside, the larva eats the food. Then it poops and spins a **cocoon** with silk that comes out of its mouth. Inside the cocoon, the larva will shed its skin again. During the time it is in the cocoon changing from a larva to an adult, it is called a **pupa**.

WORDS to KNOW

emerge: to come out.

antennae: feelers found on the head of insects and some other animals. One *antenna*, two or more *antennae*.

thorax: the middle section of an insect, where the legs and wings attach.

abdomen: the section of an insect farthest away from the head.

After about 12½ days, the pupa is done changing. The adult honey bee splits open its cocoon. It chews its way through the wax cap covering its cell and gets right to work. The time from when the queen bee lays the egg until an adult worker bee **emerges** is just 21 days.

Adult honey bees are about a half inch long. They weigh around 0.0035 ounces. That means this book weighs the same as about 2,540 honey bees!

Like all insects, a honey bee has three main sections to its body.

✻ The head is where you find the eyes, **antennae**, and mouth parts.

✻ The **thorax** is the middle section. It has two pairs of wings and three pairs of legs.

✻ The **abdomen** is the biggest part of the honey bee's body. It has a very tiny but important part—the stinger!

HEAD   THORAX   ABDOMEN

Around 20 worker honey bees could line up head to stinger on the edge of this page.

DID YOU KNOW?

 PS Watch honey bees go about their bee business with this real-time video from a camera placed on a hive in Germany.

A HONEY BEE'S HEAD

The head is the control center for a honey bee. This is where the honey bee sees, smells, tastes, eats, hears, and thinks. You do those same things, but honey bees do them a little differently.

The first thing you might notice on a honey bee's head is its two huge **compound** eyes. Each eye has more than 5,000 tiny lenses, called facets, that each see just a little bit of the world. The honey bee's brain puts all those tiny bits together to make a bigger picture. However, a honey bee can't move its eyes like you can. So even with all those lenses, a honey bee's vision is very fuzzy.

Don't feel bad that the bees have fuzzy vision. In some ways, they can see better than you. Look straight ahead of you. Without moving your head or eyes, can you see a little bit to either side? This is called your **peripheral** vision.

← OCELLI

ANTENNA

BEE'S HEAD

COMPOUND EYE

MANDIBLE

← TONGUE

The eyes of the honey bees cover most of the front and sides of their heads. This lets them see almost all the way around! They are quick to notice anything that moves, making it hard to sneak up on them.

TEST YOUR PERIPHERAL VISION

Stretch your right arm out in front of your face holding up one finger. Look straight ahead while moving your arm to the right. When do you stop seeing your finger? That's how far you can see with your peripheral vision when your eyes can't move. Next, keep your head still, but move your eyes to watch your finger. How far can you see now? Imagine how much you could see if your eyes were on the sides of your head!

honeycomb: a group of wax cells with six sides. Honey bees build honeycomb in their hive.

WORDS to KNOW

At the top of a honey bee's head, between the compound eyes, there are three small, simple eyes. Called ocelli, these eyes are used to detect light. Even on a cloudy day, a bee can use its ocelli to tell where the sun is. Knowing the location of the sun helps honey bees find their way from the hive to flowers and back again.

Near the eyes are the antennae. Each antenna is jointed like a bent elbow. Honey bees use the antennae to smell, taste, touch, and hear. The antennae are important when honey bees are inside their hive, where there isn't much light.

WHAT DO YOU CALL A BEE HAVING A BAD HAIR DAY?

HA HA HA HA HA HA

A frizz-bee!

Most insects have either a mouth that can chew on things or a mouth that can suck up liquids. Honey bees have mouths that can do both! This lets them sip nectar to make honey and chew wax to make **honeycomb**.

13

THE STORY OF THE THORAX

The thorax is the middle section on all insects. This is where the three sets of legs and two sets of wings are attached. There are also three small breathing holes along each side called **spiracles**.

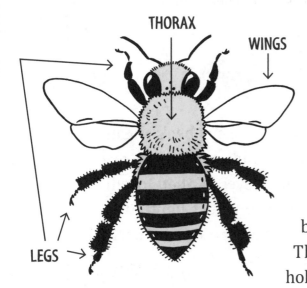

THORAX

WINGS

LEGS →

A honey bee uses its legs to walk, hold onto things, and clean pollen off the hair that grows all over its thorax. Each leg has three parts, just as each human leg has two parts. On a honey bee's front leg, there is a special part called the antennae cleaner. On each back leg, a honey bee has an area called a pollen basket. This is a group of stiff hairs that can hold 1 million grains of pollen.

Honey bees have four wings. The front wings are bigger. The smaller back wings hook onto the front wings so they all move together. Honey bees use their wings to fly in all directions—even backward! They also use their wings to fan the hive when it is hot out and to help turn nectar into honey.

When bees flap their wings, they make a buzzing sound. Honey bees can buzz different sounds. They use some of these sounds to talk to each other inside the hive.

WHY DOES A HONEY BEE HUM?

HA HA HA HA HA HA

Because it doesn't know the words!

ALL ABOUT THE ABDOMEN

The biggest section of a honey bee's body is the striped abdomen. The stripes are an easy-to-see warning for other animals to stay away. What usually happens if an animal bothers a honey bee?

Only female honey bees have stingers, which are at the end of the abdomen. Stingers are tiny, hollow tubes with a pointed tip and, usually, a **barb**. Two small sacs sit right above the stinger.

When the stinger gets pushed into skin, the sacs gets squeezed and the liquids from each sac mix together to create venom. Then when the bee flies away, the barbed stinger pulls off the end of its abdomen. This causes the bee to die.

WORDS to KNOW

barb: a sharp point going backward off another sharp point, such as on an arrow or a fishhook.

CONSIDER THE ESSENTIAL QUESTION

Write your thoughts about this chapter's Essential Question in your Bee Journal, using information you've gathered from reading and knowledge you may already have. Share it with other students and friends. Did you all come up with the same answers? What is different? Do this for every chapter.

?

ESSENTIAL QUESTION

How is a bee's body designed to do the work it's supposed to do? How is your body designed to do the work you do?

ACTIVITY

DRAW A HONEY BEE

SUPPLIES

* Bee Journal
* pencil
* eraser
* crayons or markers

One of the best ways to sharpen your skills of observation is to draw what you are studying. Even if you don't have a live bee to draw, drawing one by following these directions will help you remember the important body parts and where they belong. Draw everything in pencil first so you can erase lines you don't want.

1 Use your pencil to lightly draw a circle on the front cover of your journal. This is your honey bee's thorax.

2 Draw a flattened circle about the same size on one side. This is your honey bee's head.

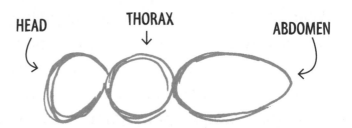

HEAD   THORAX   ABDOMEN

3 Draw a bigger teardrop shape on the other side, with the point headed out. This is your honey bee's abdomen.

4 Draw a little circle inside the top edge of the thorax to make the wing base. Draw a fat wing and a thin wing coming out of that little circle. Add some up-and-down lines to the wings to make them look shiny.

5 Draw a big oval in the middle of the head for one compound eye. Add crisscrossing lines to show lots of facets.

6 Draw three lines from top to bottom on the abdomen for a bull's eye pattern that points to the stinger. Is your bee male or female?

7 Draw two backward L's on the top of the head to make the antennae and three Z shapes on the bottom of the thorax to make your honey bee's jointed legs. Use little lines to add fuzz.

8 Ink over your pencil lines and erase any lines you don't want. Color your honey bee.

TRY THIS! Use these directions to draw some other insects. What do you notice is similar about these insects? What is different? How is drawing a honey bee useful to studying anatomy?

THE CYCLE OF LIFE

Watch a honey bee in its four stages of metamorphosis! Which stage do you think is the safest for the bee? Which is the most dangerous? How does the bee change its looks in each stage?

ACTIVITY

SUPPLIES

* 2 craft sticks
* crayons or markers
* pencil
* paper
* scissors
* toothpick
* 2 rubber bands
* Bee Journal

BEE BUZZER

Honey bee wings make a buzzing sound when they move quickly. You can make a similar buzzing sound by blowing air through this bee buzzer!

1 Decorate one side of each craft stick.

2 Trace one craft stick on the paper. Use your scissors to cut it out on the inside of the lines, so the cutout is a little smaller than the sticks.

3 Snip off two pieces of the toothpick about the same size as the width of the craft stick.

4 Put the piece of paper on the uncolored side of a craft stick. Put one piece of the toothpick on top of the paper near one end.

5 Put the other craft stick, uncolored side down, on top of the toothpick and paper, and wrap a rubber band around the stack at that end to hold it in place.

6 Slip the other toothpick piece under the piece of paper on the other end of the craft stick and wrap another rubber band around that end.

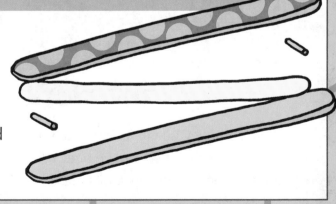

7 Hold the long edge of the craft sticks near your lips. Blow hard through the edge just as you would blow into a harmonica. What happens to the paper? What sound does it make?

TRY THIS! Try different types of paper between your craft sticks. What happens when you use really thick paper? Construction paper? Waxed paper? Record your results in your Bee Journal.

WORDS to KNOW

bee milk: a liquid food made by worker bees to feed to larvae.

YOU ARE WHAT YOU EAT

Have you heard the saying, "You are what you eat?" This is especially true for honey bees. For the first three days, all larvae are fed royal jelly. After that, most will get fed bee bread or **bee milk**. If the bees want to make a new queen, they continue to feed a few special larvae just royal jelly. The royal jelly helps the larvae grow bigger and faster, and they will all become queens. One of them will survive to rule the hive.

ACTIVITY

BARBED STINGER

SUPPLIES

* small piece of cardboard
* pencil
* scissors
* tissue paper
* Bee Journal

Have you ever gone fishing? Many fish hooks are barbed, just like a honey bee's stinger. Barbs help the hook stay in the fish's mouth. How do barbs work?

1 Use your pencil to draw a very long, skinny triangle with a pointy tip on your cardboard. This is like a queen's stinger.

2 Now draw a long, skinny triangle with a half-arrow as its tip. This is like the barbed stinger found on a worker bee or a barbed hook found on a fishing line.

3 Carefully cut out each stinger.

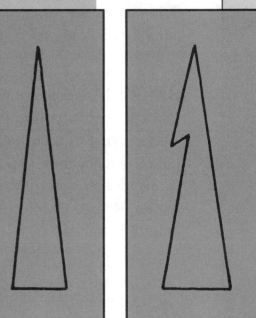

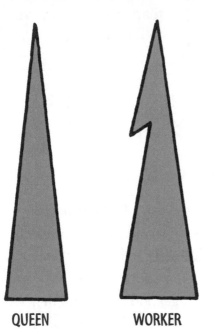

QUEEN   WORKER

4 Label the colored area of an empty page in your Bee Journal, "Stinger Tests." Which stinger do you think is going to go through and be removed from the tissue paper more easily? Write down in your journal what you think will happen.

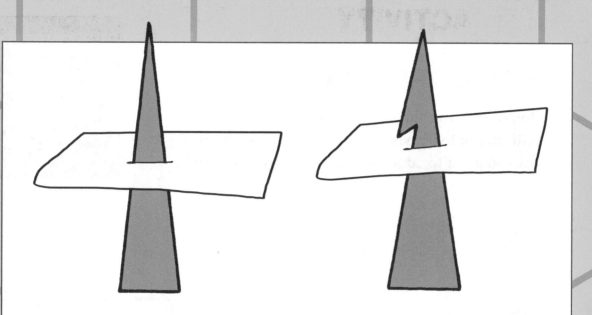

5 Poke the straight stinger through the tissue paper until there is half on each side. Gently pull it out.

6 Do the same thing with your barbed stinger. What happens? Which stinger comes out more smoothly?

7 Compare the holes made by each type of stinger. Is one larger than the other? Did the tissue paper ever tear? Write or draw your observations in your Bee Journal.

TRY THIS! What else can you poke your cardboard stingers through? Is there any material that is so thick you can't get the barbed stinger out again?

DID YOU KNOW?

Not all striped insects are honey bees. Other bees, wasps, beetles, moths, and some flies also have striped abdomens. Many of them visit flowers as well. It is safest to watch all insects from a distance to avoid getting stung.

ACTIVITY

SUPPLIES

* square piece of paper, 8½ by 8½ inches
* crayons or marker

METAMORPHOSIS MAGIC

Honey bees live through four very different stages. With this activity, you can watch a bee go from egg to larva to pupa to adult, simply by flexing your folds.

1 Fold each corner of the paper to the middle. It should look like four even triangles.

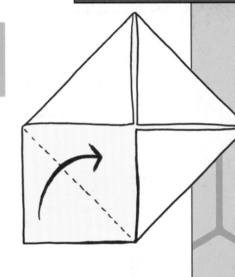

2 Turn the paper over. Fold each corner of the paper into the middle. It should look like there are eight even triangles, but they are all in sets of two.

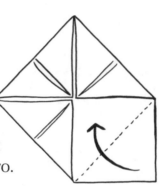

3 Lift up each set of two and draw a picture of a different life stage of the honey bee (egg, larva, pupa, adult) in each area.

4 On the inside part of the triangle that folds over the picture, write a fact about each life stage. For example, "Honey bee eggs hatch after three days."

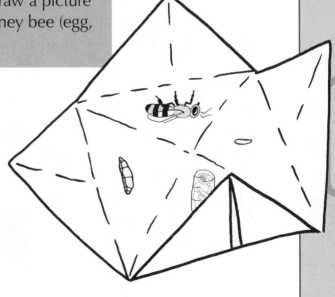

5 With the triangles folded over the pictures, flip the paper over so you see four squares. Write the names of a different life stage (egg, larva, pupa, adult) of the honey bee on each square.

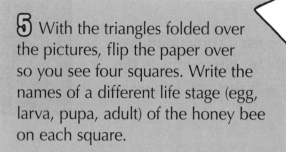

6 Fold the paper on the lines between the squares. Push up on the corners until you can fit your thumbs and first two fingers into the flaps under the squares.

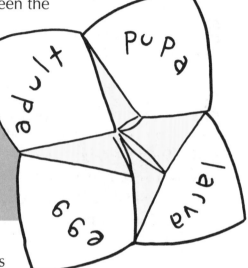

7 Practice pushing your thumbs and fingers together and apart to make it work.

8 Can your friends and family guess what life stage is under each clue?

AMAZING METAMORPHOSIS

Honey bees go through complete metamorphosis. This means there are four very different parts of their life cycle. Some insects, such as grasshoppers, go through incomplete metamorphosis. These insects never become a pupa. They just change little by little as they grow into an adult. You can watch a short movie about these two types of metamorphoses here.

SEE LIKE A BEE

Honey bees have lots of facets in each compound eye. Each facet sees things just a little bit differently. In this activity, you'll make a set of glasses that will let you see how a honey bee sees!

SUPPLIES

* ✳ 15 thin drinking straws
* ✳ scissors
* ✳ 2 rubber bands
* ✳ 3 pipe cleaners

1 Cut each straw in half. Divide the straws into two equal groups.

2 Wrap a rubber band around each bundle to hold the straws together.

3 Wrap one end of a pipe cleaner around one bundle and the other end around the other bundle, leaving a 1- or 2-inch space between bundles. This space will sit on top of your nose.

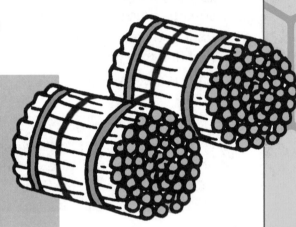

4 To attach your honey bee eye glasses to your face, wrap one end of a pipe cleaner around each bundle. When both bundles are ready, lift them up to your eyes and wrap the free end of each pipe cleaner over an ear. Now you can see like a bee!

TRY THIS! Because of their compound eyes, honey bees see in a mosaic. A mosaic is a picture made up of lots of pieces of color that look separate when you're close to them but blend to show an image when you move back. Make your own mosaic picture by putting a dot of color in each square on a piece of graph paper. How does it look up close? How does it look far away? How does it look through your bee eyes?

Honey bees are **social** animals. They live in very large groups, called colonies. In the winter, there are usually about 10,000 bees in one hive. In the summer, that number can grow to more than 50,000!

How can so many creatures live together in a space smaller than a washing machine? Part of the reason is that each type of bee has a special role. The queen, the worker bees, and the **drones** each have their own job to do.

WORDS to KNOW

social: describes animals that live in groups, rather than alone.

drone: a male honey bee.

? ESSENTIAL QUESTION

How do honey bees and humans communicate differently? Do they communicate in any similar ways?

QUEEN BEE

The queen's main job is to lay eggs. In the smallest cells of the honeycomb, she lays eggs that will become worker bees. Medium cells get eggs that will become the drones.

If the queen is getting old or the hive is getting crowded, the worker bees will make some big cells at the bottom edge of the hive. This is where the queen will lay eggs that will become queen bees. The queen knows what kind of egg to lay by walking around and feeling the size of the comb cells.

A queen bee has a very long abdomen. She also has a stinger, but it is not barbed. This is because the queen uses her stinger to lay eggs. Since it is not barbed, a queen bee can use her stinger again and again.

During the spring and summer, a good queen lays two or three eggs every minute for 12 hours a day. That can be 2,000 eggs every day! While she lays eggs, worker bees feed and clean her. When it gets cold out, she stops laying eggs. She stays in the center of the hive, eating honey and keeping warm.

DID YOU KNOW?

If you added up the weight of all the eggs a queen lays in a day and compared it to the weight of the queen, the number would be the same!

The queen bee usually lives for about 1½ years. If she dies or leaves the hive, worker bees take care of the queen larvae. As they emerge from their cells as adults, the new queen bees start to fight until there is only one left. This one

becomes the new queen. She flies from the hive with the drones so she can **mate**, and then starts doing her job of laying eggs.

DRONE BEES

Each spring, the queen lays between 100 and 1,000 eggs that become male drone bees. After the drones emerge from their cells, they spend their time eating food in the hive and waiting outside in what's called congregating areas for a queen to emerge in search of a mate. Drones do not mate with queens from their own hive. This might cause unhealthy future generations.

A new queen needs to mate to lay eggs. The drones wait in congregating areas for the new queen to take her first flights outside of the hive. She mates with up to 30 drones during these special flights. These drones die immediately. The other drones are allowed to stay in the hive until the weather gets cold and the food gets **scarce**. Then they are pushed out to die.

WORKER BEES

Worker bees have many different jobs! For the first two days after emerging from its cell, a worker bee's job is to clean cells so new eggs can be laid or new honey can be made.

When she is three days old, a worker bee stops cleaning and starts feeding bee bread to the older larvae. A few days later, her body starts to make bee milk for the youngest larvae. Or she might make the richer royal jelly for the queen larvae, if there are any.

WHAT DO YOU CALL A BEE BORN IN MAY?

HA HA HA HA HA

A maybe!

When she is about 12 days old, a worker bee's body might start to make beeswax for new cells. If she isn't busy with wax duty, she is packing nectar and pollen into the cells and taking turns fanning the nectar to turn it into honey. Some of the workers act as super heaters or coolers to keep the hive at the proper, warm temperature.

BOYS AND GIRLS

Female bees, called worker bees, are the smallest bees. Male honey bees, called drones, are a little bigger than workers and they have rounder abdomens. What else is different about workers and drones?

Between 18 and 21 days, some workers become guard bees. The guards protect the hive from **invaders**. At 21 days old, workers are ready to go outside the hive.

These workers spend six to eight hours each warm, sunny day collecting nectar, pollen, water, or propolis. A worker might fly up to 4 miles on each trip! She does this for about 21 days. By then she is six weeks old, which is about as long as a worker bee lives in the summer.

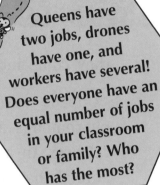

DID YOU KNOW?

Queens have two jobs, drones have one, and workers have several! Does everyone have an equal number of jobs in your classroom or family? Who has the most?

BEE COMMUNICATION

With so many bees living in one hive, they need to **communicate**. They don't talk or write like people and it's too dark in the hive to use their eyes. But bees can smell, feel, hear, and dance.

WORDS to KNOW

invader: someone who enters a place with force.

communicate: to share information in some way.

Honey bees make special chemicals called **pheromones**. Pheromones can be released into the air as a smell or as a liquid that other bees swallow. Bees change how they act and move when they come into contact with pheromones.

Queens, drones, and worker bees all make different pheromones at different times. If a bee stings an animal, it releases an alarm pheromone. Other bees will fly toward the animal that was stung and sting it too!

When the queen is young, she releases a pheromone that tells the workers they don't need to make any big queen cells. As she gets older, she makes less of that pheromone, so the worker bees build queen cells at the bottom of the hive.

SPECIAL PHEROMONE SAYS "DON'T MAKE BIG QUEEN CELLS"

DID YOU KNOW?

Many different animals make pheromones, but honey bees make more pheromone combinations than almost any animal in the world!

Honey bees also communicate with movement. When scouts find nectar-rich flowers, they return to the hive and tell the other worker bees where the flowers are—by dancing!

Worker bees gather around the scout in the honeycomb area of the hive. They can smell the nectar and pollen in her pollen basket, so they know what kind of flower she visited. By touching her with their antennae, they know how she is moving. If the flowers are nearby, she loops back and forth in what is called the round dance. The round dance lets the other bees know the flowers are no farther than one football field away, about 100 yards.

When the flowers are much farther away, the scout bee draws a map by doing a waggle dance. The bee moves in a figure eight, waggling its abdomen and buzzing its wings as it shimmies up the middle of the eight.

 Watch honey bees do the waggle dance!

The other bees smell, listen, touch, and watch the dancing bee. The waggle line tells them the direction of the flowers. The speed of the waggle tells them how far away the flowers are. The smell tells them what type of flowers to look for.

? ESSENTIAL QUESTION

Now it's time to consider and discuss the Essential Question: How do honey bees and humans communicate differently? Do they communicate in any similar ways?

ACTIVITY

BEE A QUEEN!

Each type of bee egg needs a different-size cell in the bee hive. A queen bee uses her sense of touch to decide which type of egg to lay in the cell. In real life, bee eggs are all the same size. To do this activity, you need to make bee eggs of different sizes.

1 Draw a chart like the one below on a page in your journal labeled "Bee a Queen."

2 Set the cups in the box with the smallest ones in the center, the medium ones around the small ones, and the biggest ones at the bottom. This is your honeycomb.

3 Put the caps with the eggs in front of you. Put on the blindfold—you're in a dark hive! Pretend you are the queen bee and these are your eggs. Use both hands to feel your way around your hive and around the eggs.

SUPPLIES

* Bee Journal
* pencil
* 12 cups: four each of large, medium, and small sizes
* box that can hold the cups
* bottle cap filled with uncooked rice for the worker eggs
* bottle cap filled with unpopped popcorn for the drone eggs
* bottle cap filled with dry beans for the queen eggs
* blindfold
* timer (optional)

A	B	C	D
Trial Number	Number of eggs in correct cells (+ 2 points each)	Number of extra eggs or eggs in wrong cells (– 1 point each)	Final Score (B – C)
1			
2			
3			

4 Pick one cell to start with. Keeping one hand on the cell, use the other hand to get the correct egg for the cup. Place one egg in the cup and go to the next cell.

5 After you believe you have put one egg in each cup, take off your blindfold. Count how many eggs you got into the right cup, multiply that number by two, and write that number in column B.

6 Count how many eggs you put in the wrong cup, or how many extra eggs you put in a cup, and write that as a negative number in column C.

7 Take the total from column B and subtract the total from column C. This is your final score. Record this number in column D.

8 Empty the cups and play again. Do you get better each turn? Time how long it takes you to fill the cups with the correct eggs!

TRY THIS! Put on the blindfold and ask a friend to lead you around. Can you identify the kitchen, bathroom, or hall just by the smell?

DID YOU KNOW?

There is always more than one queen larva, just in case something happens to one of them.

DOES YOUR NOSE KNOW?

Play this funny game to see if your nose can tell you what to do!

1 In your journal, make a list of your spices and smelly powders. Next to each one, write a funny action.

For example:

- "baby powder: crawl like a baby."
- "garlic: run around in circles."

2 Put a small amount of spice or other powder in each container. Cover each with a lid and put the containers in the box.

3 With your eyes closed, choose one cup, hold it away from your nose, and smell the powder inside. Don't sniff too hard! Perform the action you paired with that smell. Do you remember what it was?

TRY THIS! With a friend, take turns picking a cup for the other person to smell. If you get the action right, you get a point. The person with the most points after five rounds is the best bee!

SNIFF
SNIFF

GARLIC   ABY POW   OSEMARY

ACTIVITY

BEE BOTTOM BOOGIE

SUPPLIES

 * room with a lamp
 * friends to play eye spy

Honey bee waggling is a great way to shake your behind! The farther a bee has to fly to find the nectar, the bigger the circle it makes and the slower it dances.

1 Trace your finger around the circle below. Starting at the sun, move your finger around the right edge (red dotted line). When you reach the squiggly line at the bottom, follow the squiggle up to the sun. Continue tracing around the left edge (green dotted line) until you reach the bottom. Squiggle back up to the sun and repeat.

2 You are making a figure eight. If you were a scout bee, you would be waggling your abdomen as you moved up the squiggle. That is why it is called the waggle dance. The scout bee uses the direction of the squiggle to tell the direction of the nectar. The size of the pattern and speed of the dance tell how far away the nectar is.

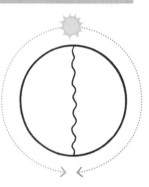

3 Now you can use the waggle dance pattern to play a game of eye spy. Instead of saying a color, you'll be dancing the directions! Stand facing a light (the sun) and look for something in the room (the nectar). Use the chart below to guide your waggle dance.

☀	Dance quickly in small figure eights	Dance at regular speed in medium figure eights	Dance slowly in large figure eights
↖↗	nectar is very close and to the left of the sun	nectar is part way across the room and to the left of the sun	nectar is far away and to the left of the sun
↔	nectar is very close and straight ahead	nectar is part way across the room and straight ahead	nectar is far away and straight ahead
↗↙	nectar is very close and to the right of the sun	nectar is part way across the room and to the right of the sun	nectar is far away and to the right of the sun

35

SUPPLIES

* masking tape
* measuring tape
* Bee Journal
* pencil

BEE PACES

Honey bees need to be able to judge how close or far away flowers are from the hive. How good are you at judging distances? You can get better by learning your pace!

1 Outside or in a gymnasium, use the masking tape to make a line about 2 feet across.

2 Put one end of the measuring tape at the line. Stretch out the measuring tape 20 feet. Mark this point with another line of masking tape.

3 Start at one line of masking tape. Count how many normal-sized steps it takes for you to get to the other piece of tape. Record this number in your journal. Repeat this two more times.

4 Add up the number of steps you took each time. Divide this number by three to find your average number of steps.

STEPS 1ST TIME + STEPS 2ND TIME + STEPS 3RD TIME = TOTAL STEPS

TOTAL STEPS ÷ 3 = AVERAGE STEPS

5 Divide 20 (the distance in feet you were walking) by the average number of steps. Your answer will be the distance you usually travel each time you take a normal step.

20 FEET ÷ AVERAGE STEPS = YOUR STEP DISTANCE IN FEET

6 To use this information, count how many steps you take between two places. Maybe it is 50 steps from your bed to the kitchen table. Multiply 50 times your step distance. That's how far it is between your bed and the table.

YOUR STEP DISTANCE × 50 STEPS = TOTAL FEET IN 50 STEPS

TRY THIS! Using your steps, measure the distance between two places, such as your chair and the door, and then use the measuring tape to see how close your estimate is.

BEE MATH!

Each worker bee that collects nectar takes about 10 trips outside of the hive each day. Each trip averages a total of 1½ miles. How many miles does an average bee fly every day?

10 TRIPS EACH DAY × 1½ MILES = TOTAL MILES PER DAY

How many miles does it fly if it collects nectar for 21 days?

TOTAL MILES PER DAY × 21 DAYS = TOTAL MILES IN 21 DAYS

If you want to really "BEE" amazed, use your average step distance from the Bee Paces activity to calculate how many steps that would be for you!

TOTAL MILES IN 21 DAYS × 5,280 FEET PER MILE = TOTAL FEET IN 21 DAYS

TOAL FEET IN 21 DAYS ÷ YOUR STEP DISTANCE IN FEET = TOTAL STEPS FOR YOU

ACTIVITY

SUPPLIES

* several kids (bees)
* 2 adjacent rooms
* 10 cups
* 4 different types of wrapped candy, 5 to 10 pieces each
* waggle dance circle chart
* light to represent the sun

SUGAR SEARCH

Put your bee pacing and waggle dance skills to the test. Can you and your friends succeed on a sugar search? In this game, one step is the same as 100 yards.

1 Name one room the bee hive and the other room the field. Place 10 cups around the field room.

2 Gather all the bees in the hive. Send one bee out to put the four sets of candies in four different cups. The cups are the flowers and the candies are the sweet nectar.

3 After the candies are placed, send out one scout bee. As soon as the scout bee finds one cup with candy, she takes one piece and flies back to the hive, counting the number of steps it takes.

4 Without talking or pointing, the scout bee waggle dances directions to the candy!

5 One at a time, the field bees go out and look for the candy the scout bee found. If the field bee is successful, it brings back one piece of candy, dances, and sends out another bee. If the field bee goes to the wrong flower, that bee must return to the hive empty-handed. The scout bee will need to dance again.

6 When the candy is gone from that cup, a new scout flies out to find a new flower and the game starts again.

CHAPTER 3
INSIDE THE BEE HIVE

The hive is the center of all honey bee activity. It's where honey bees are born and where they work, eat, and sleep.

A honey bee hive can be made in almost any hollow area that has enough room for bees to move and work. Honey bees make natural hives in trees and rock walls, under sheds, inside barrels, and even inside the walls of people's houses!

? ESSENTIAL QUESTION

Every part of the hive has a special purpose. Does every part of your house have a special purpose? How is your house like a hive?

swarm: a ball-shaped group of honey bees moving to a new hive.

hexagon: a shape with six equal sides.

WORDS to KNOW

HIVE CONSTRUCTION

When a hive gets destroyed, or if it's just too crowded, or if the queen is weakening, the worker bees decide it's time to leave. About half of the worker bees in the hive start to eat as much honey as they can. Then the queen and those fat workers fly out of the hive and make a ball of bees called a **swarm**. A few scout bees leave the swarm to go look for a new home.

What are the scout bees looking for? Honey bees need places that are above ground. They like small openings and shelter from the weather. When the scouts find a place that the queen likes, the bees fly in and the workers get busy.

Some of the worker bees make wax to build honeycomb. These are the rows of wax cells used to store honey, eggs, and larvae. Small flakes of beeswax come out of the sides of the worker bees' abdomens. They chew these flakes to make them softer and then mold them into **hexagons**.

DID YOU KNOW?

Sometimes honey bees make their homes in unusual places, such as cars, barbecue grills, boats, air conditioners, and mailboxes!

Each hexagon is called a cell. The cells are made in different sizes, depending on where they are located in the hive and what they will be used for. The worker bees attach more and more hexagons together to make their honeycomb. After about a week the bees have made enough honeycomb for the queen to start laying eggs inside the cells.

ADDING ON

When they need more room, honey bees can build up or down or start creating a new panel of honeycomb beside the first panel. Each panel is around ⅜ of an inch apart. This area is called the bee space. It's just enough room for bees to move between and around the honeycombs.

Honey bees fill the top cells and edge cells with honey. They fill the cells closer to the center of the honeycomb with pollen. Near the bottom of the honeycomb, the eggs and larvae are kept in **brood** cells. At the very bottom of the comb are the queen cells.

brood: all the eggs, larvae, and pupae in a beehive.

regulate: to control or to keep steady.

WORDS to KNOW

KEEPING WARM, KEEPING COOL

What does it feel like to be too hot? How about too cold? What do you do when you are too hot or cold in your house? Honey bees can't turn on a furnace when they want heat or an air conditioner when they want it cooler. Instead, they work to **regulate** the temperature in the hive.

Watch a speedy film of the creation of a beehive. Can you name all of the parts?

evaporate: when a liquid heats up and changes into a gas, or vapor.

water vapor: water as a gas, such as steam, mist, or fog.

WORDS to KNOW

Honey bees like their hives to be warm, around 93 degrees Fahrenheit (34 degrees Celsius). To cool things down in the summer, worker bees can bring water into the hive.

They put the water on top of the honeycomb and other worker bees flap their wings to make the water **evaporate**. When water turns from a liquid to **water vapor**, it leaves the hive and carries some of the heat away.

When the weather is too cold, the worker bees make the hive warmer. To do this some worker bees form what is called a honey bee cluster. They twitch their wing muscles, without making their wings move. This creates extra body heat that warms up the hive.

WHAT'S BETTER THAN A TALKING DOG?

HA HA HA HA HA HA HA

A spelling bee!

THE STORY OF BEEKEEPING

When people first started collecting honey, they had to visit natural beehives. To find a hive, people carefully watched bees collecting nectar and pollen. When a bee's pollen baskets are full, it flies from the flower straight back to its hive in a path called a **beeline**. People followed the beeline to find the hive.

When someone found a beehive, he had to make a hole big enough to stick his hands inside. Of course, the bees did everything they could to chase the honey thief away. Ouch!

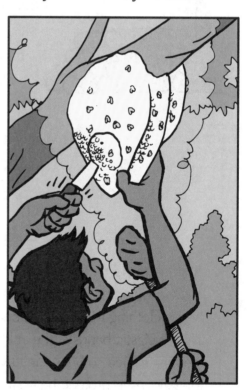

When a person collected honey, the hive was usually destroyed. What would the worker bees do if the queen was still alive after the intruder had left? They would create a swarm with the queen and find a new place to start a new hive.

Over time, people noticed that honey bees that were surrounded by smoke didn't sting. Why not?

In nature, when a hive is on fire, the honey bees know they need to leave and find a new place to live.

When worker bees smell smoke, they hurry to fill their bellies with honey. The bees are so busy that they don't worry about intruders. Smoke also covers up the alarm pheromones made by guard bees. People started using smoking branches or pots when they raided beehives.

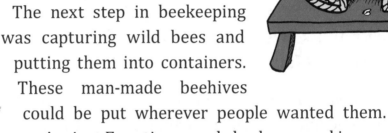

The next step in beekeeping was capturing wild bees and putting them into containers. These man-made beehives could be put wherever people wanted them. Ancient Egyptians used clay boxes and jars as beehives. People in Medieval Europe wove skeps, which are upside-down straw baskets. Beekeepers in Africa used clay pipes.

BEE SUIT

Another important step in the history of beekeeping is the development of the bee suit. This is a piece of heavy clothing that covers a beekeeper's entire body. Ties or elastic bands at the ankles and wrists keep the clothing sealed so bees can't fly in. Beekeepers also wear long gloves to protect their hands. A hard hat with a mesh veil protects a beekeeper's head.

BEEHIVE DESIGNS

Beekeepers tried different ideas to make their own beehives. These ideas included hanging honeycomb from sticks that could be lifted out of hives, or stacking boxes on top of each other with the queen in the bottom and the honey on top.

DID YOU KNOW?

Beehives can be found on every **continent** except Antarctica.

All of these **cavities** kept the honey bees safe, dry, and nearby. However, beekeepers still had to break apart the hives to get the honey out. Then it took a long time for the bees to build new honeycombs and start making more honey.

cavity: an empty space inside a solid object.

continent: one of Earth's largest land areas.

super: a special box with no top or bottom that is used to hold frames of honeycomb.

WORDS to KNOW

In 1851, an American named Lorenzo Langstroth designed a beehive with 10 wooden frames inside a box. Each frame could be removed and had a ⅜-inch space on each side. Multiple boxes were stacked together, and the top box was called the **super** and the lower box was called the brood. A lid on top kept the super protected.

There are many advantages to this style of hive. A beekeeper can puff smoke into the hive and lift out one frame at a time to make sure the bees are healthy. The beekeeper can check to see if the queen is still laying eggs and that the bees have enough honey. The beekeeper can also keep the frame out to get the honey.

More supers can be added to the beehive as the bees fill up the frames. In the winter, beekeepers can help the bees stay warm by wrapping the beehives with blankets. The Langstroth hive is the design used the most around the world today.

? ESSENTIAL QUESTION

Now it's time to consider and discuss the Essential Question: Every part of the hive has a special purpose. Does every part of your house have a special purpose? How is your house like a hive?

AROUND THE WORLD

Most of the honey in the United States comes from North Dakota, South Dakota, Montana, California, and Florida. You can even find **managed** beehives in Alaska and on the tops of buildings in New York City.

Check out some other places you can find beehives in the United States. This map was created by volunteers and is not complete. It doesn't show beehives in North and South Dakota or in Montana.

ACTIVITY

HONEY EXTRACTION

SUPPLIES

* 2 paper cups
* hole punch
* scissors
* string
* water
* Bee Journal

How do beekeepers get the honey out of the honeycomb? First they use hot knives to cut off the wax caps. Then they put the frames in machines called extractors. An extractor is a spinner with walls to keep the splashing honey inside. See how this works by becoming your own spinning machine. This is best done outside on a warm day!

1 Punch three holes at equal distances around the top edge of each cup.

2 Cut six pieces of string about 15 inches long. Tie one end of a string in each hole. Tie the three free ends of string together for each cup.

3 Fill each cup about halfway with water and gather the free ends of the string for one cup in each hand.

4 Bend your arms at the elbows and start twirling your entire body in a circle. Let the cups rise up so they are stretched out to your sides. What happens to the water?

TRY THIS! Design and draw your own honey extractor. What keeps the frames inside? Do you want the honey to spray toward the middle or toward the outside wall? What makes it spin? How do you get the honey out of the machine?

ACTIVITY

SUPER STRENGTH TEST

SUPPLIES

* ✳ ruler
* ✳ pencil
* ✳ copy paper, 8½ by 11 inches
* ✳ scissors
* ✳ tape
* ✳ Bee Journal
* ✳ books of equal weight

Honey bees need their comb to be waterproof, strong, and recyclable! The shape needs to hold their babies, honey, and pollen. It cannot waste space and it must be easy to clean. See if you agree with honey bees that a hexagon is the best shape to use in a beehive.

1 Use the ruler and pencil to divide the paper into eight long strips, each 1 inch wide and 11 inches long. There will be a strip of paper a half-inch wide left over. Cut out each strip.

2 Use two strips to make two separate circles. Bend the strips around and tape the ends together.

3 Use two more strips to make two separate squares. Starting at one end of each strip, measure and mark lines 2½ inches apart. Crease each strip at these marks and tape the ends to make two separate squares.

4 Use two more strips to make two separate triangles. Starting at one end of each strip, measure and mark lines 3½ inches apart. Crease each strip at the marks and tape the long end over on each triangle.

HOW DO BEES BRUSH THEIR HAIR?

With honeycombs!

5 Use the last two strips to make two separate hexagons. Starting at one end of each strip, measure and mark lines 1¾ inches apart. Crease each strip at the marks and tape the long end over.

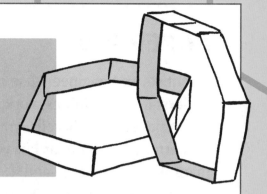

Shape	Books supported standing up	Books supported lying flat
Circle		
Square		
Triangle		
Hexagon		

6 Draw a chart like the one above in your journal. Place one of each shape on its side on a table and one standing up. Which shape do you think will support the most books without being crushed to the table? Draw a star in that shape's box.

7 Place one book at a time on top of each shape. What happens? Add more books to the shapes that are still standing until they are crushed flat. Record the number of books each shape holds on your chart. Was your prediction correct?

TRY THIS! Trace around each shape on a piece of graph paper. Color in the squares that fit into each shape. Which shape has the largest colored area? Why is this important in a beehive?

THINK ABOUT IT: Look for circles, triangles, squares, and hexagons in buildings, bridges, and other structures. Engineers are the people who use science, math, and creativity to design and build these structures. Why do engineers choose these shapes?

ACTIVITY

PAPER HIVE

Scientists and engineers use models to better understand how things work. Using the spaces on graph paper as your cells, you can make a model of a modern beehive. Record in your journal how long it takes to do steps 2, 3, and 4.

SUPPLIES

* 10 sheets of graph paper or hexagon paper found at incompetech.com
* scissors
* gold, yellow, and brown crayons
* 10 hanging file folders
* timer
* pad of small sticky notes
* box that fits hanging file folders

1 If you download a pdf of hexagon graph paper, have an adult help you. Set the hexagon size at 0.1 or 0.2 inches, then download and print. Fold each sheet of graph paper in half.

2 Start the timer. On half of the sheet, color the cells around the edges gold, for honey. Color the rest of the cells on that half of the sheet yellow, for pollen.

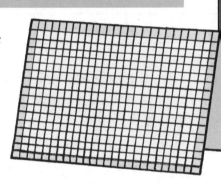

3 On the other half of the sheet, color the cells around the edges gold for honey. Draw a light brown bee egg or bee larva, which looks like a short, fat worm, in each of the remaining cells on this half of the sheet. These are the brood cells. Your colored piece of graph paper is your honeycomb.

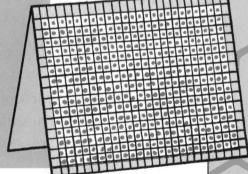

4 Color each piece of graph paper like this and place them, colored side up and out, in the hanging file folders. These are your frames. Stop the timer.

5 You are going to draw the bees of the hive on separate small sticky notes. Remember, there is only one big queen bee! Draw a few drones, but make most of your bees worker bees.

It takes honey bees about 11 pounds of honey to make one pound of wax. Whenever possible, honey bees reuse cells or recycle wax. To recycle wax, they chew up pieces of old cells or cell caps and form it into new honeycomb.

6 Stick a few bees on each piece of graph paper and hang all the frames from the edges of the box. The box is your super. Open each folder and see how each honeycomb looks.

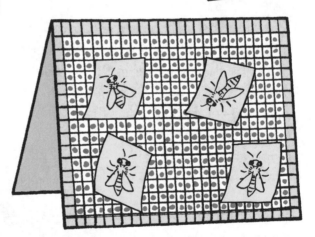

7 Imagine you are a beekeeper from long ago. Remember, they destroyed hives to get the honey out. Take out a paper frame, crumple it up, and throw it away. Look at your journal and figure out how long it will take you to make a new frame. How much time would it take to make five new supers (boxes) with 10 frames (hanging file folders) each? Think of all the hours the bees would need to make a new hive!

ACTIVITY

CLUSTER AND TWITCH

To keep warm in the winter, honey bees huddle their twitching bodies close together. How does that help?

SUPPLIES

* journal
* pencil
* 15 to 20 fabric or yarn balls, or rolled up socks
* box that will hold the balls close together
* hair dryer
* timer
* thermometer
* red pen
* blue pen

1 Label a page in your journal "Cluster and Twitch." Draw a graph like the one on the next page. Put the temperature on the vertical line. Put the time on the horizontal line.

2 Imagine each fabric ball is a really big bee. Place all the balls in the box to make a model of a honey bee cluster.

3 Warm the balls with the hair dryer for three minutes. As soon as you turn the hair dryer off, place the thermometer in the middle of the cluster. Check the temperature every 30 seconds. Record the temperatures in red ink on your graph at the correct time.

4 After three minutes, put your hand in the box and move it around. Where does it feel the warmest? Where does it feel the coolest?

5 Spread the balls out on the top of a table. Use the hair dryer for two or three minutes to warm them.

52

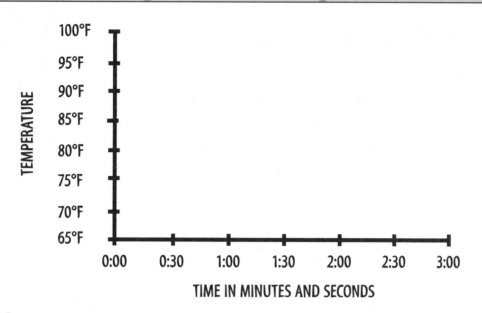

6 As soon as you turn the hair dryer off, place the thermometer on the middle of the table.

7 Check the temperature every 30 seconds for three minutes. Record the temperatures in blue on your graph at the correct time. After three minutes, feel the balls. Do any of them feel warmer than the others?

8 Connect the red dots. Connect the blue dots. Compare the two lines. What do the lines tell you about the better way to stay warm?

MOVING IN THE CLUSTER

In a honey bee cluster, the worker bees constantly change places. Bees near the middle move toward the edge while bees near the edge move toward the middle. Why do you think they do this?

ACTIVITY

EVAPORATION STATION

In the summer, thousands of bees spend a lot of time flapping their wings without going anywhere. Their job is to move air around in the hive. This moving air picks up water from the comb and nectar cells. As the water evaporates, the hive cools down and the nectar thickens and becomes honey.

1 Draw a large honey bee wing on the stiff paper.

2 Cut out the wing and glue one end of it to the craft stick.

3 Cut the paper towel into two strips. Get both strips damp, but not dripping wet.

4 Feel how warm your forearm is. Then place one damp paper towel strip over each forearm.

5 Wave your wing over the paper towel on only one arm for as long as you can. You will get tired!

6 As soon as you stop waving the wing, feel the paper towel on that arm. Feel your skin under the paper towel. Then feel the other paper towel and your other arm. Which arm feels cooler? Which paper towel feels drier? Why is one paper towel drier? Record your observations in your journal.

DID YOU KNOW?

While flying, a honey bee beats its wings around 200 times each second!

What are honey bees best known for? Honey, of course!
People have eaten honey for thousands of years.
Honey gives us energy, and people also use honey
in their hair, on their skin, and even as medicine. If
honey is kept in sealed containers, it won't **spoil**.

Since it used to be difficult and dangerous to raid a wild
beehive, people didn't want to waste anything they took. They
found ways to use everything, including the honey, beeswax,
propolis, royal jelly, and even the bee venom.

WORDS to KNOW

spoil: to rot and become
dangerous to eat.

? ESSENTIAL QUESTION

Do you use any bee products?
How would your life be different
if you didn't have this product?

Honey bees are responsible for more than just the products they make. As honey bees go about their business collecting nectar and pollen from flowers, they help spread around the pollen. Why is this important?

Pollen is made in the male parts of a flower. Flowers need help getting the pollen to the female part of the flower so the plant can make seeds. This is called pollination. Without honey bees, broccoli, cantaloupe, almonds, and many other food crops would not be pollinated and would not make seeds.

DID YOU KNOW?

When you eat an apple, peach, or pear, you are eating a seed package! Cut one open and see.

POLLINATION

Plants make seeds with their flowers. To make seeds, flowers need to get all the right parts together, especially the **ova** and the pollen. These are both tiny but very important to the process of making seeds. The ova and the pollen grow on different parts of the flower. On some plants, the ova and pollen grow on different flowers!

The ova are found in a little sac in the middle of the flower called an **ovary**. The only way for things to get in and out of the ovary is through a long tube called a **style**.

At the top of the style is a flat, slightly sticky landing place called the **stigma**. All three parts together are the **pistil**. These are the female parts of the plant.

WORDS to KNOW

ova: the eggs of a flower.

ovary: the sac that holds the ova at the bottom of the style in a flower.

style: the tube in a flower that goes between the stigma and the ovary.

stigma: the somewhat flat, sticky pad found on top of the style in a flower.

pistil: the female parts of a flower, including the ovary, stigma, style, and ova.

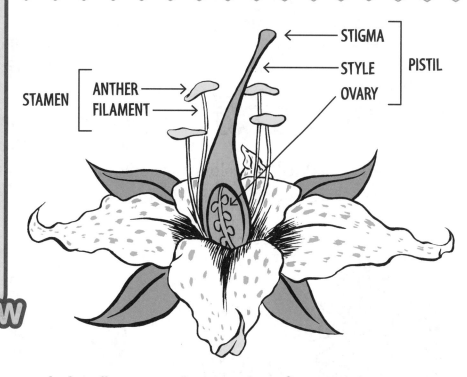

stamen: the male parts of a flower, including the filament, anther, and pollen.

filament: the thin stalk inside a flower that holds up the anther.

anther: the part of a flower that makes and holds the pollen.

WORDS to KNOW

The male parts of the flower make up the **stamen**. This includes a thin stalk called a **filament** and the **anther**, which lies on top of the filament. The anther is where you find the pollen.

How do the ova and the pollen come together to make a seed? Some pollen is light enough to rely on the wind to carry it to the ova. Other pollen needs to catch a ride on an insect or an animal.

When an insect or animal visits a flower, it usually gets some pollen on it. When the insect moves, some pollen drops off. If the pollen lands on the stigma and the pollen and ova come together, the flower will make seeds. When those seeds drop into the soil or are planted by a farmer, new plants with flowers will grow.

57

ultraviolet: a kind of light with short wavelengths. It can't be seen with the human eye.

WORDS to KNOW

Some flowers produce smells that attract animals. Others have big petals that are easy for insects to land and stand on. Some flowers have designs that point toward the pollen. These are in **ultraviolet** colors that only bees and other animals can see. These designs are called bee signs.

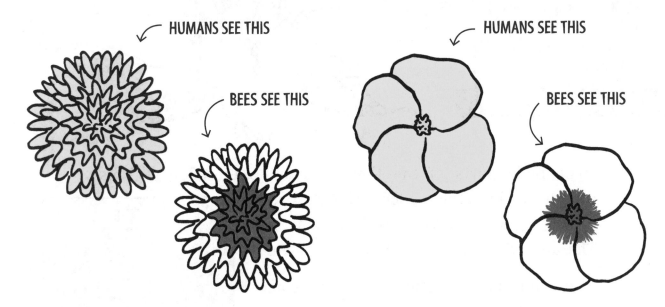

HUMANS SEE THIS

BEES SEE THIS

HUMANS SEE THIS

BEES SEE THIS

ULTRAVIOLET COLORS

Honey bees can't see red, but they can see other colors that we can't see. These colors are called ultraviolet. All colors are made of light waves. Ultraviolet light waves have a shorter wavelength than the light waves visible to people. There are ultraviolet colors in many flowers, butterflies, birds, and fish.

MAKING HONEY

Honey bees start making honey while they're flying back to the hive! Here's how.

At the flower, a bee uses its **proboscis** to suck up the nectar. The nectar is found in different places on different flowers. From there, the nectar goes into the bee's two stomachs.

The nectar that goes into the first stomach gives the bee energy to work. The nectar that goes into the second stomach gets made into honey. Inside the second stomach are special chemicals called **enzymes**. These enzymes mix with the nectar while the bee is flying back to the hive.

proboscis: the sucking mouthpart of honey bees and some other insects.

enzyme: a natural chemical that causes a reaction.

archaeologist: a scientist who studies things made and used by people who lived long ago.

WORDS to KNOW

ANCIENT HONEY

Archaeologists have found honey and pictures of ancient bee hives inside the pyramids in Egypt. Even though some of the honey is more than 5,000 years old, it is still okay to eat! How is this possible? Honey has very little water in it, which means it stores well for a long time. If the container is sealed tightly enough, no air or water can get in it. Then the honey will keep for a very long time—thousands of years, in fact!

At the hive, the bee moves the nectar-enzyme mixture up and out of its stomach. It gives the mixture to another bee to put into a honey cell. Other bees add more nectar-enzyme mixture. As the younger bees fan the cells, water evaporates from the mixture and it thickens. When the cell is full and most of the water is gone, a worker will put a wax cap on top. The honey is done.

DID YOU KNOW?

One of the most expensive spices in the world is saffron. It is made from the pistils of a special type of crocus flower.

GETTING STUNG STINGS

Have you ever been stung by a bee? Ouch! First you feel a sharp poke and then a hot, red, itchy bump forms. For about 3 percent of the population, getting stung by a bee is extremely dangerous.

WHAT'S WAXY?

Beeswax is another useful bee product. Bees use it to build a strong, waterproof honeycomb for storing their food and their brood. People use beeswax to make many things, such as candles, lip balm, and waxed thread.

Look around your house for waxy items, including wax paper, waxed dental floss, candles, crayons, lip balm, lipstick, and furniture polish. Put a drop of water on a piece of wax paper. What happens to the water? Hold a crayon tightly in your fist for two minutes. Will it bend without breaking? What **properties** does wax have that would be useful to bees? Why is wax useful for people?

WORDS to KNOW

property: a characteristic of something. The way something is.

If you are allergic to bee venom, your throat can swell up and you can find it hard to breathe. People who know they are allergic to bees carry around Epi-pens, which are needles that give them the medicine they need right away.

Each female worker bee makes about $\frac{2}{10}$ of a milligram of venom. It would take more than 2 million honey bees to make a pound of venom. Bees use venom for protection. It doesn't work on all hive raiders, but it does work on most. Scientists collect bee venom to study it with the hope of finding a way to use it as a medicine.

? ESSENTIAL QUESTION

Now it's time to consider and discuss the Essential Question: Do you use any bee products? How would your life be different if you didn't have this product?

DOCTOR BEES

How can bee venom be a weapon for bees but a medicine for doctors? Stings get red and itchy because the ingredients in bee venom change how the body works. The venom creates tiny holes in some cell walls. These holes make it easier for things to move in and out of the cells. Your blood reacts to the venom by releasing fluids to try to flush the venom away. While the venom is getting flushed away, so are the things coming out of the cells. If some diseases are in the cells, they could get flushed away as well. There is no proof that this could really act as a medicine, but it might! It's why scientists are doing more research.

ACTIVITY

JUMBO FLOWER MODEL

Most flowers only bloom for a short time each year. Some flowers, such as amaryllis, have big parts that are easy to see. Other plants, such as dandelions and clover, have much smaller parts. You can make a flower with large parts to model the process of pollination.

1 Cut the paper lunch bag about halfway down each corner. Fold out the four pieces and color them. These are the flower petals.

2 Pour juice or another sweet drink into the bottle. The liquid should be about 1 inch deep. This is the nectar inside the ovary at the base of the style. Place the bottle inside the bag.

3 Cut the sticky parts out of the Post-it notes. Tape them around the opening of the bottle, with the sticky side facing out and up. These make the stigma. You now have the female part of the flower, called the pistil.

4 Take four small pieces of clay. Roll the pieces into balls and then flatten each ball. Stick the blunt end of one skewer into each piece of clay. The skewers are the filaments, one of the male parts of the flower. Place the skewers in the bag, standing on their clay ends. Each filament should be along a different side, so they are surrounding the pistil.

5 Stick a Cheeto on the top of each skewer for the anthers with their pollen. Together, the filaments with their anthers make the stamens, the male parts of the flower.

6 Put the bottle cap about 18 inches away from the bag. This is one cell of the honeycomb.

7 Use the straw as your proboscis! Stick the straw into the bottle and then put your finger over the top end. Lift your hand without taking your finger off the end of the straw.

8 Fly your hand over to your bottle cap. Take your finger off to release the nectar into the honeycomb cell. Go back to the flower to get more nectar and record how many visits it takes to fill your bottle cap with nectar.

THINK ABOUT IT: Look at the paper around the top of the bottle. Is there any pollen on it? How did it get there? Why is this important?

PEOPLE AND POLLEN

In the summer, when there are lots of flowers blooming, you might breathe in more than 1 million pollen grains each day. In some people, the body treats pollen as an invader. To flush the pollen out, the body creates lots of fluids, including snot and tears. These fluids are made and stored in the head. For people who suffer from pollen allergies, this means a stuffy head, runny nose, and watery eyes. Since honey has pollen in it, some people believe they can teach their bodies that pollen is NOT an invader by eating honey made by local bees.

ACTIVITY

POLLEN POWER

SUPPLIES

* Bee Journal
* ruler
* pencil
* black paper
* 5 powders such as flour, baby powder, cinnamon, or other spices
* 1/8 teaspoon
* small bowls or cups
* straw
* clear tape
* 5 cotton swabs

All flowers need pollen to make seeds. Some pollen is light and smooth enough to be carried by the wind. Other flowers produce pollen to be carried by insects and other animals. This pollen often has little spikes to help it stick to insects. Flowers have **adapted** to use their surroundings. What kind of **habitat** does a flower with light pollen live in? What kind of habitat might a flower with spiky pollen live in?

1 In your journal, create a chart like the one below to record your observations.

2 You are going to try different things with each of the powders and observe what happens. Make predictions about each powder. Which one will travel the farthest on a puff of air? Which will stick best to your skin? Which will stick best to a cotton swab? Make a star in the box on the chart that matches your predictions.

Powder	Distance traveled by air	Sticks to skin	Sticks to cotton swab	Would be best moved by
Flour				
Baby Powder				
Cinnamon				

WORDS to KNOW

adapt: changes a plant or animal makes to survive in its environment.

habitat: the natural area where a plant or animal lives.

3 Put the black paper on a table in an area with no wind. Keep the short edge closest to you. Place the ruler next to the paper and mark a line half an inch from the edge closest to you. Label this area "Powder Pollen Area." Place ⅛ teaspoon of one powder in the starting area. Place ⅛ teaspoon of the same powder in a small cup.

4 Place the tip of the straw near the pile of powder. Blow one quick small puff of air through the straw. Record how far the pollen travels.

5 Dip your finger quickly in and out of the cup of powder. Roll your finger around on the sticky side of a piece of clear tape to show how much powder stuck. Place this tape in the correct box on your chart.

6 Dip the cotton swab quickly in and out of the cup of powder. Roll it around on the sticky side of a piece of clear tape to remove the powder. Place this tape in the correct box on your chart.

7 Repeat steps 4 to 6 for each powder. Record your results on the chart. Were your predictions correct?

THINK ABOUT IT: Look at each powder with a magnifying lens. Which powders look as though they are going to travel more easily by air? By animal? Why?

WHAT DID THE BEE SAY TO THE NAUGHTY BEE?

HA HA HA HA HA

Bee-hive yourself!

ACTIVITY

CALLING ALL BEES

Bees can see more colors than you can because they can see ultraviolet (UV) light. Flowers make patterns with UV colors that lead honey bees and other pollinators to the middle part of the flower. This activity is best done on a warm, sunny day that isn't too windy.

1 Use regular markers to color the edges of the sheets of paper. Do it exactly the same way you colored the edges of the pages in your Bee Journal when you made it.

2 In a bowl, mix one spoonful of sugar with four spoonfuls of warm water. Stir until the sugar is dissolved.

3 Find a table or other flat area outside. Fan out the pages of your Bee Journal in a circle. The highlighted edges of your journal will make a design that will lead honey bees to your bowl.

4 About 1 foot away from your Bee Journal, use the colored edges of the paper (from step 1) to make the same design.

5 Put a small bowl down in the middle of each design. Put a sponge in the middle of each bowl. Pour in enough sugar water to make a small puddle in the bottom of the bowl.

6 Leave the bowls alone. It may take a few hours or even a day or so for the bees to find the bowls. Put more sugar water in each bowl if it dries out.

7 Which bowl is the first one the bees find? Do they seem to like one bowl better? What happens if you change the pattern of the colored edges?

DID YOU KNOW?

Because of their sensitive sense of smell, honey bees have been trained to work as bomb detectors!

BEE METEOROLOGISTS

Honey bees sometimes act as **meteorologists**! A honey bee will not leave its hive if it is cooler than 50 degrees Fahrenheit (10 degrees Celsius). They are also sensitive to changes in the air pressure. A drop in air pressure usually means a storm is coming. If you see a bunch of bees heading back to their hive in the middle of the day, you might be in for a storm!

SUPPLIES

* balloon
* scissors
* drinking glass
* rubber band
* straight pin
* spoon
* baking soda
* water
* 1 small paper or plastic cup
* 2 medicine/ eye droppers
* vinegar
* Bee Journal
* pencil

STING REACTION

Honey bee bodies have two small sacs right above the stinger. When the stinger gets pushed into skin, the sacs gets squeezed and the liquids from each sac mix together to create venom.

CAUTION: Have an adult help you with the sharp pin.

1 Cut around the edge of the balloon to make two equal-sized pieces that will fit over the drinking glass to act like skin.

2 Stretch one piece of the balloon over the top of the drinking glass. Keep it in place with the rubber band.

3 Use the pin as a stinger to poke a small hole in the top of the balloon.

4 Mix one spoonful of baking soda and two spoonfuls of water in a cup. Stir well.

DID YOU KNOW?

It takes worker bees about 10 million trips to flowers to make one pound of honey! In three weeks of foraging, 12 worker bees will make about a teaspoon of honey.

BEE-MADE MUMMIES

Have you ever touched the bark of an evergreen tree and gotten sticky resin on your hand? Honey bees collect that resin from the buds of certain trees and carry it back to their hives. They mix it with wax and some enzymes and then use it as a very special type of glue. Propolis glue not only holds things together, it also makes things waterproof and kills germs! It is also a great mummy maker. When small animals get into a bee hive, the bees can kill it with stings, but can't carry it out. So they cover it with propolis. Many people believe that ancient Egyptians studied these bee-made mummies and used some of the same methods to make their own mummies.

5 Fill one dropper with vinegar. Fill the other dropper with the baking soda mix. The droppers are models for the sacs near the stinger in a honey bee.

6 Push the tips of both droppers through the hole in the balloon stretched across the drinking glass. At the same time, give both of them a squeeze so about half of the liquid comes out of each dropper. What happens? How is this similar to a human's reaction to a bee sting? How long does the reaction last?

TRY THIS! The longer the stinger is in, the more venom gets pumped under your skin. What happens if you squeeze the rest of the liquids out of the droppers?

ACTIVITY

SWEET SNACK BARS

Honey tastes great by itself, on toast, or in tea. It also is fun to use in recipes.

CAUTION: Have an adult help you when handling hot things.

1 Pour the cereal in the large bowl and set it aside. Spray the pan with cooking spray and set that aside.

2 In the microwave-safe bowl, stir together the honey, peanut butter, and milk powder. Heat the mixture in the microwave on high heat for 30 seconds. Stir and heat again until it's blended well. Be careful and use the hot pads when handling the bowl.

3 Stir the mixture into the cereal until everything is coated. Pour it into the square pan and use the back of the spoon to press it down evenly.

4 Let the bars cool. Cut into 12 squares and enjoy!

TRY THIS! Experiment with some substitutions. Can you use oatmeal instead of rice cereal? What happens if you add some nuts, sesame seeds, or raisins? Get creative.

SUPPLIES

* measuring cup
* 4 cups toasted rice cereal
* large bowl
* 8-by-8-inch pan
* cooking spray
* microwave-safe bowl
* ½ cup honey
* ½ cup chunky peanut butter
* ½ cup nonfat dry milk powder
* spoon
* microwave
* hot pads
* butter knife

70

Honey bees have lived on Earth more than 100 million years. This is as far back as the time of the dinosaurs and longer than people have lived on Earth! Honey bees have survived ice ages, when ice covered much of the planet, and a **meteor** strike that killed all the dinosaurs.

WORDS to KNOW

meteor: a rock or chunk of ice that falls toward Earth from space. Small meteors burn up before they reach Earth and we see them as shooting stars.

forage: to collect food in the wild.

orbit: to move in a constant circle around something.

When people moved honey bees to new continents, the bees adapted and found new flowers to **forage**. Honey bees even built honeycomb while **orbiting** Earth on NASA's space shuttle.

? **ESSENTIAL QUESTION**

Why is it important to help honey bees remain healthy and alive?

71

During all these years, honey bees have changed very little. But now, scientists and beekeepers believe honey bees are in trouble. Since 2006, there has been an increase in cases of entire colonies of honey bees suddenly dying. This is a condition called Colony Collapse Disorder (CCD).

WHAT DO YOU CALL A HONEY BEE ON A SPACE SHIP?

HA HA HA HA HA HA

Buzz Lightyear

Scientists have some ideas about what causes CCD, but no one is positive about what is happening. Do you have any ideas?

We depend on honey bees for some of our food. There will probably always be at least some honey bees somewhere on Earth. But what if too many bees die at the same time? A lot of the flowers that need pollination to turn into food will not get pollinated. That would mean less food for us to eat.

THREATS TO BEES

What are some of the **threats** that honey bees face? What can you do to help protect against those threats and save the honey bees?

Every part of the world has it's own weather and climate. The weather is what is happening today or this week. Is it snowing at your house today? Raining? Maybe it's a beach day! The climate is what happens to the weather year after year. In Boston, Massachusetts, it is cold in the winter and often snowy, while in Tampa, Florida, the winters are sunny and warm.

WORDS to KNOW

threat: a person or thing that can cause danger or damage.

Honey Bees in Trouble

Climate change is a shift in the earth's weather systems. This has happened in many different places during the past few years. It affects temperature, rain and snowfall, sea levels, and how many storms develop.

climate change: changes to the average weather patterns in an area during a long period of time.

atmosphere: the blanket of air surrounding Earth.

WORDS to KNOW

We burn oil and gas and coal—called fossil fuels—to heat or cool our homes. We also use fossil fuels to run our cars and make electricity. Burning these fossil fuels releases a gas called carbon dioxide into the atmosphere.

Too much carbon dioxide in the atmosphere traps the sun's heat. It warms the air and the oceans. This causes climate change.

WHAT YOU CAN DO

Climate change is a huge challenge that many people are working on solving. It's hard to get people to change their habits and burn less fossil fuels. You can help by being a good citizen of Earth. Plant and water a flower garden to help feed the bees. Walk or ride your bike instead of riding in a car whenever possible. Try to create less trash. Recycle your trash or find creative ways to use it again! Can you think of other ways to help the environment?

Climate change is not the same everywhere. Some parts of the world are growing colder and wetter. Remember, honey bees don't like to go out of the hive when it is cold and wet. If they don't go out, they can't collect nectar and pollen for their food.

Other parts of the world are getting hotter and drier. Plants have a hard time growing flowers if it is too hot and dry. If there are no flowers, honey bees can't find any nectar and pollen.

Perhaps the worst threat to honey bees is mites. People often move plants and animals to new places. Sometimes people do this on purpose and sometimes they do it by accident. Some of these plants and animals are not good for honey bees. A tiny creature called a varroa mite feeds on honey bees, in the same way that mosquitoes feed on people.

DID YOU KNOW?

Eighteen states in the United States have named the honey bee as their official insect. Is your state one of them?

VARROA MITE

WHAT YOU CAN DO

To help reduce the number of new pests and diseases that attack honey bees, be sure to garden with plants that are **native** to your area. Don't move plants or animals to different countries or even to different states!

WORDS to KNOW

native: a plant or animal that is naturally found in a certain area.

Varroa mites were first found only in Asia, where they fed on Asian honey bees. They don't seem to bother these bees too much. But people moved European bees to Asia and Asian bees to Europe.

When European honey bees came to North America, some of them became infected with varroa mites. The mites feed on the European bees so much that it makes them weak. Honey bees have a lot of work to do and weak bees can't do much work. If too many bees get infected, the hive dies.

Another problem for bees is the chemicals that are used to kill insects. These chemicals kill off both the plant-eating insects and the honey bees.

Some people spray or swat every insect they see. They might know that honey bees help their garden, but they might not know how to tell honey bees apart from the bee mimics.

WORDS to KNOW

mimic: a plant or animal that looks like another plant or animal.

This syrphid fly looks like a honey bee, but it isn't! Can you spot some differences?

Why do other insects want to look like honey bees? One reason is protection. What happens when an animal gets stung by a honey bee? An animal who has been stung will probably leave all honey bees alone, as well as honey bee mimics.

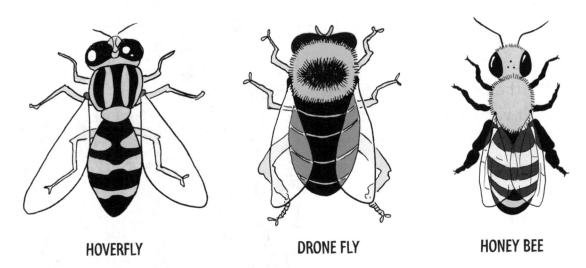

HOVERFLY   DRONE FLY   HONEY BEE

Take a good look at the insect pictures above. Can you list three ways each mimic is different from the honey bee? Try to find one difference in each body section—the head, thorax, and abdomen.

WHAT YOU CAN DO

Learn to recognize bee mimics so you aren't tempted to swat a real honey bee. Ask your parents not to spray chemicals in the garden, so the honey bees stay safe. Try to eat **organic** food that hasn't been sprayed with chemicals.

WORDS to KNOW

organic: food grown naturally, without chemicals.

Honey bees don't eat other insects. Some insects that do eat other insects mimic honey bees. Why? To lull other insects into thinking they're safe. When those other insects get close, the honey bee mimics catch them and eat them!

HONEY BEES AND HUMANS

Honey bees and humans have lived side by side for thousands of years. With the help of humans, honey bees have expanded their range and can now be found in most places in the world. With the help of honey bees, humans have expanded the amount of food they produce so more people can eat.

Now people are worried about the health of honey bees and humans. Is the world changing too much and too fast? Are the pests and problems that bother honey bees a warning that humans need to change what they do to the natural world? Many people think so.

WHAT DO YOU CALL A WASP?

HA HA HA HA HA HA

A wanna-bee!

By now, you have learned about many things you can do to make the world a better place for both people and honey bees. You can plant a native garden, avoid spraying insects, and try to use less energy every day. It would "BEE" awesome if you helped honey bees thrive!

? ESSENTIAL QUESTION

Now it's time to consider and discuss the Essential Question:
Why is it important to help honey bees remain healthy and alive?

ACTIVITY

FLOATING MIST

One reason honey bees are in trouble is because a lot of people spray chemicals to kill insects they don't want. Some of these people might like honey bees, but don't realize that the spray they are using kills or injures all types of insects.

1 Cover the floor with the large sheets of paper and stick it in place with tape. This will be your garden or farm. Put the plant in the middle.

2 Divide the sticky notes into four equal piles. For one pile, color a honey bee on each sticky note. Color a mosquito on each sticky note in another pile, a caterpillar on each sticky note in another pile, and a beetle on each sticky note in the last pile.

3 Stick one sticky note on each craft stick. Make a base for each stick with a small ball of clay. Place the insects all around the paper garden.

4 Fill the spray bottle almost full with water. Add 3 or 4 drops of food coloring and mix well.

SUPPLIES

* large sheets of paper or a white, plastic tablecloth
* masking tape or duct tape
* plant
* 20 sticky notes
* crayons
* 20 craft sticks
* clay
* spray bottle
* water
* food coloring
* fan
* measuring tape
* pencil
* Bee Journal

5 Which insects do you want to eliminate from your garden? Mosquitoes can drink your blood. Caterpillars might eat the leaves of your plants. Some beetles can pinch you! Use your bottle to spray the animals you don't want in your garden.

6 Measure how far the spray travels around each animal. Count how many other insects were accidentally sprayed. Record your data in your Bee Journal with a chart like the one below.

	How many bugs accidentally sprayed	How far spray traveled
No Fan		
Fan		

7 Set the fan in one corner and turn it on high. Repeat the experiment and compare your observations. Do you think people should spray on a windy day? What are some other ways they can manage insects?

RING, RING!

Do you use a smartphone? For a time, scientists wondered if the electronics in smartphones were bothering the bees. After doing research, they discovered that although honey bees can sense the vibrations created by smartphones, the phone buzz doesn't seem to cause much trouble. In fact, some scientists are now trying to use old smartphones to help honey bees by keeping track of their activities!

PLANT A HONEY BEE GARDEN

If you plant flowers that make lots of nectar and pollen, honey bees are certain to find them. If you can, plant flowers that bloom at different times so the bees will have nectar during spring, summer, and fall!

1 If you are using a plastic food container, punch some holes in the bottom so the extra water can run out. Put the lid under the container after you punch the holes.

2 Fill the container almost full with soil.

3 Use the nail to poke holes about ⅓-inch deep. Drop one or two seeds in each hole.

4 Gently press soil over the top of the seeds. Water and place in a warm, sunny area.

5 Check the soil every day. When it feels dry, add water. If the weather is warm, move your plants outside when they start to grow.

SUPPLIES

* flower pot or plastic food container with lid
* soil
* nail
* flower seeds (see chart on page 81)
* water
* Bee Journal
* pencil

6 Record in your journal when the plant starts to grow and bloom. Note when you see honey bees or other insects flying around your plant. How often do they visit? How long do the flowers bloom for?

WHAT DO YOU GET IF YOU CROSS A SKUNK WITH A BEE?

A stinky stinger!

Wondering which flowers to plant? Try these!

Spring	Summer	Fall
Sweet William	Zinnias	Asters
Petunias	Salvias	Marigolds

FLOWER TIPS

Sometimes you can trick a plant into making more flowers.

✳ As soon as a flower starts to die, cut it off the stem. This is called dead heading. The plant might grow a new flower.

✳ You can also try pinching off the tops of your stems if they start to get long. This will make the plant produce more stems and look fuller.

ACTIVITY

BEE FRIENDLY

Most people know that honey bees are helpful insects and they don't want to hurt them. Sometimes all they need is a sign telling them to "BEE" aware and help the honey bees.

1 Use a page in your Bee Journal to jot down your ideas for a poster. What do you want it to say? Here are some ideas to get you started.

* Bee Nice! Don't spray me, I'm making honey.

* Bee Aware! Honey bees need you to care.

* Like fruit? Thank a honey bee!

2 Use your pencil to sketch on the poster board. Where do you want the words on your poster? Draw or cut out some magazine pictures to add to it. When you find a design you like, make it permanent with markers and glue.

3 Put the poster in your window or nail it to the stake and put it outside.